Jesus is Alive!

Jesus is Alive!

*The Story of Easter and
Why it Matters So Very Much*

by Pastor Mike Sager

Publishing
Angel
Climbing

Jesus is Alive!
Written by Pastor Mike Sager

Transcribed and edited by Lisa Soland
Text copyright © 2023 Mike Sager

Published in 2023 by:
Climbing Angel Publishing
PO Box 32381
Knoxville, Tennessee 37930
http://www.ClimbingAngel.com

First Edition: April 2023
Printed in the United States of America

Cover photo: Shutterstock
Graphic Design: Climbing Angel Publishing

ISBN: 978-1-956218-25-1
Library of Congress Control Number: 2023904197

To the Cousins...
James, Angela, Will, Joy, Erik, Jaime,
Steve, Calvin, Kristi, Karl, and Luke.

Thanks for such great times together,
making our family memories so much richer!
I'm sure Grandma Corinne would love for you
to take to heart the message of this book.

1

The Single Sermon Series

PRAYER

Thank you, Father, as we spend time in Your Word, for the opportunity to worship You without fear of persecution. We have many freedoms and we want to make the most of them. As we read, we ask that you speak to each one of us, where we are with what specifically we need to hear from you. Only you can do that, Lord, and we trust you. Whether we are studying alone or in a group, we ask that you show yourself to us through these words. Keep us sensitive to your Spirit so that we can sense what You are prompting. And Lord, give us that faithful response of obedience to whatever you reveal. Thank you, God, that you are with us as we read. Thank you for this moment right now. What a special time to celebrate this tremendous truth of your love and power demonstrated through Christ our Lord, through His life, His death, and certainly through the resurrection. We ask now that You would do what you would choose to do for each one of us. We ask this in Jesus' name. Amen.

EASTER CHOCOLATE

Every year about this time, I notice a change in one of the grocery aisles of my supermarket. Down that aisle filled with holiday goodies, I see chocolate for sale, most of which is formed in the shape of a bunny rabbit with long ears. My personal favorite is the one-pound chocolate bunny filled with peanut butter. I have always enjoyed Reese's Peanut Butter Cups, but at Easter time, I get to enjoy the combination of the flavors in bunny form.

Perhaps you have noticed them on the shelves of your local store. Maybe you, too, find yourself walking by the fresh chocolate bunnies and hear them calling out your name. It's part of the way our culture celebrates this special holiday weekend.

When I was a child growing up, whenever I thought of Easter, I thought of candy—Easter egg hunts and jelly beans decorated in spring colors, particularly pink, bright green, and yellow. As adults, perhaps we think of families gathering together and sharing elaborate meals with those we love.

Now those things are great; there is nothing

wrong with them. But there is something truly special and unique about Easter Sunday. That same chocolate bunny will be on sale the day after Easter for half price. So why is Easter so special? Let us take a look at what makes this particular holiday so extraordinary.

If you talk to believers in Christ, they would say that Easter, for Christians, is the most important day of the year. Why is that? Well, it's because of the resurrection and everything that it encompasses. If you are a follower of Christ, there is no doubt that you are familiar with the resurrection. I pray that as we read through this book and remind ourselves of the significant events that took place during that original Easter weekend, it will greatly encourage you.

If you are not a follower of Christ and are not familiar with what it means to be committed to Jesus, day by day, then I invite you to read ahead. We will explore the significance of this day and what the resurrection represents to us all. You might ask yourself, "Why should I? Why should I invest the time?" And the reason is simple—the resurrection is the most momentous event in all of history.

When the Church first started, the people of God had been used to gathering on the Sabbath (Saturday). But today, the Christian church at large gathers on Sunday. What instigated that change from Saturday to Sunday? Why do so many believers worship on Sunday? Well, it's all because of what we will study in this little book. We now worship on Sunday because of Jesus' resurrection. The day He came back from the dead. That changed everything.

In the gospel accounts, there is "a lot of ink" regarding that final week of Jesus' life. Depending on which gospel you're reading, as much as a quarter to one-third of each book focuses on the last week of Jesus' life. We call it Passion week or Holy week. In it God demonstrates his passion or love for us through what Jesus gave us when He sacrificed himself on the cross.

The gospel of John 20:1-18 contains many details of that first day of the week when Jesus was resurrected.

AN EMPTY TOMB

Now on the first day of the week Mary Magdalene came to the tomb early, while it was still dark, and saw that the stone had been taken away from the tomb.
(John 20:1)

Early on Sunday, the first day of the week, John tells us, "While it was still dark...." So, it was very early in the morning when Mary

Magdalene *came to the tomb*. By the way, *Magdalene* is not Mary's last name. It describes where she is from—the city or village of Magdala, a town on the West side of Galilee. So she is a Galilean. By this, we know that Mary Magdalene came to Jesus or was introduced to Jesus very early in His ministry. This Mary is the same woman we read about in Luke, Chapter 8:

> *Soon afterward he went on through cities and villages, proclaiming and bringing the good news of the kingdom of God. And the twelve were with him, and also some women who had been healed of evil spirits and infirmities: Mary, called Magdalene, from whom seven demons had gone out...*
> (Luke 8:1-2)

We don't know what Mary's issues were; there were many, no doubt. Some would say Magdala is a community where all kinds of sin existed, including prostitution. Perhaps Mary Magdalene was involved in prostitution; we don't know for sure. She lived a difficult and sinful life and found forgiveness and freedom in Christ. Jesus freed her from the demonic repression under which she suffered. Her life is an excellent portrayal of someone deep in sin, stuck in the ways of this world, who then came to freedom in Christ.

Mary Magdalene had a remarkable relationship with Jesus. If you want to see this relationship visually portrayed in a special way, look at the series entitled *The Chosen*. This series is not only about the life of Christ but also focuses on many others who were impacted by Jesus' life. In it, Jesus spares Mary's life and transforms her in the process. The series is a great tool in helping us visualize the gospel. If you're unfamiliar with *The Chosen*, I recommend that you watch it. (At the time of this publication, the series has completed three seasons and is available streaming on all of Angel Studios' platforms.)

The other three gospels, Matthew, Mark, and Luke, tell us that a group of women came together with Mary. But from John's account, it appears Mary arrived at the tomb first. The first thing she noticed is that the stone had been rolled away.

In those days, in that region, many were buried in tombs, something like a cave. Inside, they would carve out what looked like a bench. They would then set the corpses on those benches.

Jesus was placed in a tomb that had not yet been used. It was sealed by rolling a stone in front of the entrance. These stones weighed tons. They were extremely heavy, and to move them would require several people.

On their way to the tomb, the women asked themselves, "Who is going to move the stone for us?" And that was a good question. Mary gets there, and the stone is moved already. She looks in and finds that there is no body. In verse 2, we see that she runs to Simon Peter. (In fact, there is a lot of running going on in this passage.)

So she ran and went to Simon Peter and the other disciple, the one whom Jesus loved, and said to them, "They have taken the Lord out of the tomb, and we do not know where they have laid him."
(John 20:2)

John doesn't name himself in his Gospel. Instead, he refers to himself throughout as "the one Jesus loved..." perhaps as a humble way of talking about himself.

PETER AND JOHN

So Peter went out with the other disciple, and they were going toward the tomb. Both of them were running together, but the other disciple outran Peter and reached the tomb first. And stooping to look in, he saw the linen cloths lying there, but he did not go in.
(John 20:3-5)

John was the youngest of the disciples, which might be why he outran Peter to the tomb. It is interesting, though, that this is mentioned. You might say they ran to the tomb, and John won the race. In fact, John mentions it twice. I don't know if this is a guy thing or something else altogether. Mary is still back a ways as the two disciples run to the tomb. Notice, the Bible says John looks in and sees "the linen cloths lying there, but he did not go in. Then Simon Peter came, following him, and went into the tomb. He saw the linen cloths lying there..." (John 20: 5-6)

The words "to see" or "saw" are translated from different words in the original language. In verse 6, when it refers to Peter who "saw the linen cloths," the term "saw" is where we get the word "theorize." In other words, "saw" means that Simon Peter was processing.

Then Simon Peter came, following him, and went into the tomb. He saw the linen cloths lying there, and the face cloth, which had been on Jesus'[a] head, not lying with the linen cloths but folded up in a place by itself. Then the other disciple, who had reached the tomb first, also went in, and he saw and believed; for as yet they did not understand the Scripture, that he must rise from the dead.
(John 20:6-9)

Now, remember, these disciples are not expecting Jesus to be alive. Jesus told them He would rise from the dead, but as we hear John say, they didn't understand that. So John sees the strips lying there, and it's not as if they have been torn and are lying all over the tomb. They're simply lying there.

In first-century Judaism, when they would prepare someone for burial, they would wrap the arms, legs, and body, place a shroud or cloth over the face, then set them in the tomb. Peter and John saw the linen strips lying there with no body inside them. And then, the face cloth was rolled up or folded and set aside. The picture we get is as if the material just deflated. Looking at the scene, you would think, "What in the world happened here?" And that's the point, right? It doesn't look like anybody struggled to get out of the cave. And it doesn't look like somebody entered the cave and ripped the linens off the body. There's no evidence that someone just came in and stole everything. Jesus' body is gone, but the strips are still there. Clearly, something unique has taken place.

*Then the other disciple, who had reached the tomb first, also went in, and he **saw** and believed; for as yet they did not understand the Scripture, that he must rise from the dead.*
(John 20:8-9)

This time the word "saw" has a different meaning. Here it means that John was *perceiving* and *realizing* something. He sees something, and now the dots begin to connect in his mind. Notice what it says, "He saw and believed." So, what did John believe? Well, the Bible doesn't say. But the next part of the verse gives us good insight. John says in verse 9, "...for as yet they did not understand the Scripture, that he must rise from the dead." Perhaps "they" refers to the disciples at large. They knew the Old Testament. They knew Scripture. But they did not understand that Jesus had to rise from the dead.

Let's look at the Apostle Paul's words in 1 Corinthians 15:3-4. This book is written to the church of Corinth years after Christ walked the earth, and Paul is writing about the resurrection. Apparently, there were people in Corinth, even in the church itself, saying that the resurrection did not happen and feeling that the resurrection wasn't important anyway.

For I delivered to you as of first importance what I also received: that Christ died for our sins in accordance with the Scriptures, that he was buried, that he was raised on the third day in accordance with the Scriptures...
(1 Corinthians 15:3-4)

The entire life of Christ, including His resurrection, was predicted and documented in writing hundreds of years before it happened. The prophecies of the Old Testament fulfilled in the person of Christ are a remarkable testimony to the authenticity of the Old and New Testament. Anyone can write a book and say, "This is God's Word, and this is what it says." But how do we know it's true? Part of knowing that the Bible is true involves becoming familiar with the writings of the prophets, penned hundreds of years before Christ and then fulfilled in Him. But there is one anticipated event that demonstrates the power of God and the reliability of His Word and promises and that is the resurrection.

Throughout 1 Corinthians 15, the Apostle Paul writes about Jesus' resurrection. (Please take a moment to read the entire chapter.) If the resurrection is not real, and we celebrate Easter simply because we like the holiday, then we are wasting our time.

When people say, "I don't care if the gospel is true or not. Living for others is better, and I want to live that way regardless," the Apostle Paul would respond by saying, "Baloney." If you are living for other people sacrificially, and the resurrection isn't true, then you're living simply for *this* life and wasting your only opportunity. But if the resurrection *is* true and there is an eternity to look forward to, then what we do in Christ's name for the sake of others is an investment in our experience in eternity. Jesus' resurrection demonstrates what happens to us *after* this life, which is very good. That's why Paul ends the chapter by saying this:

> *Therefore, my beloved brothers, be*
> *steadfast, immovable, always abounding*
> *in the work of the Lord, knowing that in the*
> *Lord your labor is not in vain.*
> (1 Corinthians 15:58)

However, if the resurrection isn't real, then eat, drink, and be merry because this life is all you've got.

We live in the light of eternity. How do we know that eternity is true? How do we know what is going to happen next? We know because of Jesus' life, death, and resurrection. We know because of the promises of Scripture. The resurrection is what validates the message of the Bible. The Old Testament is all about the Messiah, the redeemer. It foretells God's redemption for us through the person and work of His Son, Jesus Christ.

JESUS APPEARS TO MARY

> *But Mary was standing outside the tomb,*
> *weeping; so as she wept, she stooped to look*

into the tomb; and she saw two angels in white sitting, one at the head and one at the feet, where the body of Jesus had been lying. And they said to her, "Woman, why are you weeping?" She said to them, "Because they have taken away my Lord, and I do not know where they put Him."
(John 20:11-13 NASB)

The disciples look, and John believes, but they didn't understand completely what was happening, so they go back home. And then we have Jesus' appearance to Mary. Mary has returned to the tomb and is crying. She is devastated. Not only is Jesus dead, but now she doesn't even know where His body is. She looks into the tomb and sees two angels in white sitting there—one where Jesus' head was and the other where His feet were.

The other gospels in the Bible describe those angels as men, but "angels" simply means "messengers of God." They appear as humans and are in *white*. In other words, there is some sort of glory or whiteness in how they are dressed or how they appear. The angels ask her, "Woman, why are you weeping?" It's an interesting question to ask someone who is at a gravesite. What's the point? What the angels are getting around to sharing with Mary is: "You don't need to cry. There's not the loss here you think there is."

Mary says, "Because they have taken away my Lord, and I do not know where they put Him."

By the way, who is the "they?" I don't know. It's that proverbial "they." When talking with each other, we often say, "Well, you know what *they* say." That's what occurs here when Mary says, "Because **they** have taken away my Lord..." Mary knows something has happened to the body. She's expecting to find a corpse. She's expecting to find a dead body and it's not there. So, what's her conclusion? *They* took it, which is wrong. Isn't it?

Having said this, she turned around and
saw Jesus standing, but she did not know
that it was Jesus.
(John 20:14)

Mary turns around and sees Jesus but she doesn't know it's Him. Why not? I don't know; she's been crying; she's in trauma. Mary is grieving, of course. Or maybe it's simply that Jesus hasn't been revealed yet. But assuredly, what she finds at the tomb is not meeting her expectation. She doesn't expect to find Jesus standing and talking with her. So, she thinks He's the gardener or whoever takes care of the place. And she says, "Sir, if you have carried him away, tell me where you have laid him, and I will take him away" (John 20:15). I think that's grief talking; I don't know, but this is not what she expected.

Now, notice how Jesus responds. He doesn't say, "Mary, it's me," revealing Himself to her. What does He do? He speaks her name —"Mary" and immediately she recognizes Him.

> Jesus said to her, "Mary." She turned and said to him in Aramaic, "Rabboni!" (which means Teacher). Jesus said to her, "Do not cling to me, for I have not yet ascended to the Father; but go to my brothers and say to them, 'I am ascending to my Father and your Father, to my God and your God.'" Mary Magdalene went and announced to the disciples, "I have seen the Lord"—and that he had said these things to her.
> (John 20:16-18)

I think of John 10:27, "My sheep hear my voice, and I know them, and they follow me." Mary recognizes Him. In fact, she turns to Him and cries out, "Rabboni," which means teacher. That is what she would have called Jesus when she followed him—the Teacher. And Jesus says to her, "Do not cling to me..." which is interesting. We're not told what happened, but can you imagine? Mary probably gives Him a huge bear hug because she is so surprised that He is alive and so very happy to see Him. She acts like she probably won't let Him go, so Jesus says, "Don't hold onto me. I've not yet returned to the Father."

In John 14:25-26, Jesus taught His disciples in the Upper Room:

> *"These things I have spoken to you while I am still with you. But the Helper, the Holy Spirit, whom the Father will send in my name, he will teach you all things and bring to your remembrance all that I have said to you."*

Jesus explains to them that it's good for Him to go away because when He goes away, the Father will send another Helper like Jesus, except He won't just be *with* them; the Holy Spirit will be *in* them. God, Himself, will indwell the believer. Paul tells the Ephesian church that the Holy Spirit is given to us as a pledge, a guarantee of our future.

> *In him you also, when you heard the word of truth, the gospel of your salvation, and believed in him, were sealed with the promised Holy Spirit, who is the guarantee of our inheritance until we acquire possession of it, to the praise of his glory.*
> (Ephesians 1:13-14)

When we entrust ourselves to Christ, He gives us His Spirit. Everyone who entrusts himself to Jesus receives *Him*, and He's with them always, all the time, through the end of the age.

TELLING OTHERS

Jesus said to her, "Do not cling to me, for I have not yet ascended to the Father; but go to my brothers and say to them, 'I am ascending to my Father and your Father, to my God and your God.'"
(John 20:17)

Following the resurrection, Jesus still has work to do. He remains on earth for about 40 more days, occasionally appearing to His disciples. Look what he says, "...but go to my brothers and say to them, 'I am ascending to my Father and your Father, to my God and your God.'" Interesting.

Perhaps people read the Bible, the story of Christ, and they write it off as a myth. Maybe they say to themselves, "It's a nice idea, but there is no reality to it. The disciples must have made it up. Jesus died, and when people die, they die. The disciples must have made up that Jesus returned from the dead."

Many things go against that thought process, and one of them is found in the Bible. Mary Magdalene was not exactly an upstanding woman in the community. *And she's a woman.* In no way is this meant to offend modern women. But in the first century women were treated much differently than they are today. If you are going to make up a story and want any credibility to it, you would not use a woman as the first to witness the resurrected Christ.

In the book *The Final Days of Jesus*, authors Andreas J. Kostenberger and Justin Taylor put it this way: "If you were going to make up a story but wanted to make it credible, you wouldn't choose women as the first public witnesses," which all of the gospels do. They continue, "Jewish women could offer testimony in domestic, family, and private law but would not function this way as public witnesses or public spokesmen. The Jewish historian Josephus wrote that even the witness of multiple women was not acceptable 'because of the levity and boldness of their sex.'" That is how the culture of that time treated the words of women.

There was a critic of Christianity, a man by the name of Celsus, who wrote against the gospel. In the second century, this Greek philosopher mocked the idea of Mary Magdalene being a resurrection witness, referring to her as a "hysterical female."

If this story of the resurrection is made up, the last thing you would do is choose for a witness someone who would not be credible to those reading it. Why would anybody choose

Mary Magdalene as the first witness to see the resurrected Christ and go tell others? Simple. Because it's true. Because it's real. Because this is the way it happened.

So, what is the significance of the resurrection? What is the meaning of Easter to you? These are important questions, but not just because we're discussing what occurred on the original, first Easter Sunday. These are important questions because of what they signify today.

Easter validates the message of the scriptures. And what is the overall message of the scriptures? First, there is one true God—a spiritual, divine being who created everything, physical and spiritual. God created it all. He made the Universe. In fact, on this planet Earth, God made what we call *humanity*. And He created humanity *in His image*.

> So God created man in his own image,
> in the image of God he created him;
> male and female he created them.
> (Genesis 1:27)

Why is that important? Because this creature ("male and female he created them"), made in God's image, can relate to Him. There's a personal relationship available. And He gave this creature the ability to choose, to make choices. We call it free will. And this creature chose to disobey. Even though God had warned this creature, "...but of the tree of the knowledge of good and evil you shall not eat, for in the day that you eat of it you shall surely die" (Genesis 2:17).

Did they physically die? Well, when sin entered into creation, they started dying physically. Adam and Eve were tempted by a fallen angel, a messenger of God that rebelled against God. He brought sin into this "creature's" life, into humanity. And when we sinned against God, that fellowship with God was broken. We are made in His image, but that image is now marred with sin. You can call it selfishness, pride, arrogance, or ego; call it whatever you'd like. Most people recognize that nobody's perfect. Right? But consider the ramifications of that reality. Because we're not perfect, because we're not righteous, when we die, the Bible tells us:

And just as it is appointed for man to die once, and after that comes judgment,
(Hebrews 9:27)

At the end of your life, you will stand before the Judge—God himself—and there will be one thing you will need if you want any hope for that meeting, and that is righteousness. And you don't have it. I don't have it. But God did not leave us in that hopeless state, just awaiting His judgment. That's why the Messiah came.

"Messiah" means the anointed one and is the Old Testament name for Jesus. The New Testament term is "The Christ"—the one who would be the redeemer. Ever since that creature, made in His image, fell, the rest of the story consists of God pursuing that creature—calling that creature back into fellowship with Himself. God sent His prophets and messengers, calling His people back. He chose a people, a nation—Israel—to share who God is with the rest of the world. But they didn't do so well. And they disobeyed. God promised that He would send a redeemer, a savior, and that's why we celebrate Christmas. Christmas is the celebration of the birth of the Savior because you and I need saving.

We are separated from God, and when we die, we will face His judgment. What we need is righteousness. We don't have it. Where are we going to get it? Well, that's why Jesus came. Jesus was born of a virgin and He had no sin. He lived His whole life fulfilling God's standard of righteousness.

Take any religious leader in the world you choose, of any time period. By their own admission, they are not perfect—only one possesses righteousness. There's only one place for you and me to get righteousness, and that is from the righteous One. When we entrust ourselves to Him, believe in Him, and follow Him, He takes our sins upon Himself at the cross. Then He takes His righteousness and places it on us, and I can now stand in the righteousness of Christ, having no fear of God's judgment. I have new life in Him, simply by faith, and I live in light of that reality. That's what it means to believe.

In Romans 10:9, Paul put it this way to the Roman church, "...if you confess with your mouth that Jesus is Lord...." This does not mean you say the words, and that does it. It means that you recognize that Jesus is boss. He is God in the flesh. He is the one I need to follow.

...because, if you confess with your mouth that Jesus is Lord and believe in your heart that God raised him from the dead, you will be saved.
(Romans 10:9)

Jesus Christ conquered death. He lived a righteous life. He taught the truths of God. He demonstrated the power of God in the miracles He performed. He demonstrated the love of God, especially in the way He died. When Jesus died on the cross, He not only suffered crucifixion, which many had before and after him, but He also took on the wrath of God, the punishment of God for the sins of humanity. When Jesus cried out on the cross, "My God, my God, why have you forsaken me?" it wasn't because the nails in His hands hurt (Matthew 27:46). It was because He was taking on the penalty of the sins of humanity. Then Jesus died and was placed in a tomb. And as the scripture predicted, three days later, Jesus came back to life. Death could not conquer Him. This is what the scripture teaches and has taught for hundreds of years. Those prophesies were fulfilled in the life of Christ.

Friends, that is our hope. All of us will face death. What's on the other side? How do you know for sure? Look at the person and the life of Christ. He was raised with a new body.

When the perishable puts on the imperishable, and the mortal puts on immortality, then shall come to pass the saying that is written:
"Death is swallowed up in victory."
"O death, where is your victory?
O death, where is your sting?"
(1 Corinthians 15:54-55)

"And the mortal puts on immortality, then shall come to pass the saying that is written: 'Death is swallowed up in victory.'" Our bodies are not going to last for eternity. We need to take on a new body.

The scripture says when I die, if I am in Christ, my spirit goes to be with the Lord. My body goes into the ground or wherever it goes, but my spirit is with Jesus. At the resurrection, my new body will be reunited with my spirit, and I will be with Christ forever.

There's this thing called "a new heaven" and "a new earth."

*Then I saw a new heaven and a new earth,
for the first heaven and the first earth had
passed away, and the sea was no more.*
(Revelation 21:1)

There will be no more sin in the *new heaven* and the *new earth*. That is reality. How do we know that? Because of Jesus Christ. He said, "I am the way, and the truth, and the life. No one comes to the Father except through me" (John 14:6). That is either true or not. If it's not true, we are wasting our time. If it's true, there is nothing better to focus on because it gives us hope in this life. It gives us purpose and significance *in this life* and *in the life to come.*

This is the gospel message. If you are a follower of Christ, I trust that this truth is encouraging to you. The resurrection reminds us of the reality of the gospel message.

If you are not a follower of Christ, let me share this scenario* with you. Think about receiving an envelope in the mail. We're not talking about an email or a message sent to you through social media. You actually get an envelope in the mail, and it looks official. In fact, it's from a law firm. And you open it up, and you see that the letter is from an attorney. The letter says you have a relative you didn't know about, and that relative died and left you millions of dollars. What would you do with the letter? There are so many scams today, so maybe you crumple it up and throw it away. I don't think so. Wouldn't you at least look into it? Investigate? If so, why? Because it's *millions of dollars*. If it's real, that is valuable.

The resurrection points to something far more significant than millions of dollars. Won't you at least look into it? If you are not a follower of Christ, check out the life, the ministry, the death, and resurrection of Jesus Christ. American author, Lee Strobel, has written a couple of books on the subject: *The Case for Christ* and *The Case for the Resurrection*. Those two books would be a great place to start. You can also go to the website *www.GotQuestions.org*. This is a great resource for you to get answers to questions that might arise as you move forward.

Look into what we celebrate on Easter. If

you're not sure of it, if you're not aware of it, or if you're skeptical, I get it. But it is so valuable; do not ignore it. And if you want to chat with me sometime, I would be happy to talk with you, as would nearly any pastor of a Gospel oriented church. Perhaps we could share a big chocolate bunny together.

We celebrate Easter because of what is called *The Good News*. We celebrate Easter because Jesus Christ has given us life, and He has given it to us abundantly. Not one of us deserves what Jesus did for us on the cross. None of us can earn it. It can't be bought. It's a gift of God.

Listen for His voice because Jesus will call you by name. He wants you to know Him. He died so you could have freedom from sin, guilt, and shame. He died so you could have freedom to live with purpose and significance in a broken world. There are a lot of people today looking for hope and significance. Only one person has provided that for us, and His name is Jesus.

* An illustration from Pastor Timothy Keller.

ABOUT CLIMBING ANGEL PUBLISHING

Climbing Angel Publishing exists for the purpose of sharing stories of hope and encouragement, aiding in the gathering together of community, and supporting the process of betterment. The following books are available at ClimbingAngel.com and major bookstores.

ADULT BOOKS: (Romans 8:28-30)

In His Image, by Sam Polson
(English, Romanian, & Mandarin)
By Faith, by Sam Polson (English & Romanian)
My Birthday Gift to Jesus, by Lisa Soland
Without Ceasing, by Dr. Dennis Davidson
SonLight: Daily Light from the Pages of God's Word,
by Sam Polson
Corona Victus: Conquering the Virus of Fear,
by Sam Polson
Art Bushing: His Diary, Letters, & Photographs of WWII,
by Art Bushing
Art & Dotty: His Diary, Their Letters & Photographs of WWII, by Art Bushing
Trimisul, by Stan Johnson (Romanian)
Life Changing Prayer, by Sam Polson
The Climbing Angel Christmas Treasury, variety of authors
J. Calvin Coolidge: Letters from the Korean War
Stories from Kingman, AZ: The Heart of Historic Route 66,
by Loren B. Wilson

Pathways: Ancient Paths from the Pages of the Old Testament by Sam Polson
Jesus is Alive! by Mike Sager
My Mother's Bible, by Sam Polson

CHILDREN'S BOOKS: (Philippians 4:8)

The Christmas Tree Angel, by Lisa Soland
The Unmade Moose, by Lisa Soland
Thump, by Lisa Soland
Somebunny To Love, by Lisa Soland
(English & Mandarin)
The Truth About God's Rainbow, by Lisa Soland
God's Promises, by Lisa Soland
The Boy & The Bagel Necklace, by Lisa Soland
God's Hands and Feet, by Lisa Soland
I Like To Be Quiet, by Joni Caldwell
Wheels Off!, by Karlie Saumier
Ella's Trip of a Lifetime, by Melanie Ewbank
Because You Are Mine, by Gayle Childress Greene
Jeremy Plays the Blues, by Amy Oden Simpson
Bad Hair Day, by Jasmyne Simpkins
I Like To Read, by Joni Caldwell
Trunks Up!, by Karlie Saumier
Perusha's Paradise, by Bette Reed Smith
Ruby and the Treasure Within, by Tonya Celeste Hobbs
Abby, the Wonder Dog & her Warrior Princess,
by Melanie Ewbank
The Christmas Coat, by Lisa Soland